Grand & Arsenal

Grand &

Winner of the Iowa Poetry Prize

Arsenal

by Kerri Webster

UNIVERSITY OF IOWA PRESS

Iowa City

University of Iowa Press, Iowa City 52242
Copyright © 2012 by Kerri Webster
www.uiowapress.org
Printed in the United States of America

Design by Richard Hendel

The University of Iowa Press is a member of
Green Press Initiative and is committed to preserving
natural resources.

A special thanks to Jane Mead, the 2011 Iowa Poetry Prize judge.

Printed on acid-free paper

ISBN-13: 978-1-60938-091-5
ISBN-10: 1-60938-091-6
LCCN: 2011938440

For Kathleen Finneran

Did you know that every chair in this room is stuffed
with the hair of horses I've loved?
— *Murder at the Gallop, MGM, 1963*

About halfway to River Heights, while enjoying the
pastoral scenes of cows standing knee-high in shallow
sections of the stream, and sheep grazing on flower-dotted
hillsides, Nancy suddenly realized the sun had been
blotted out.
— Carolyn Keene, *The Secret of the Old Clock*

She looked like someone had just set her favorite city on fire.
— Kelly Link, "The Hortlak"

Contents

Acknowledgments

Thanks to the editors of the journals in which these poems appeared: *Antioch Review*: "Keeper, Keeper"; *At Length*: "Atomic Clock"; *Bat City Review*: "Postscript"; *Boston Review*: "Seed Vault"; *Denver Quarterly*: "Ecophilia" and "All the Way from Here"; *Drunken Boat*: "Sea Voyage"; *High Chair*: "Tinnitus," "Thrift," and "Places I Haven't Slept"; *Horse Less Review*: "Foretold" and "Implanted Memories"; *Kenyon Review*: "Oracle Weather"; *poetrysociety.org*: "The Book of Matthew"; *Super Arrow*: "Vernal, Utah," "Little Ornaments," and "Polysemy"; *Washington Square Review*: "Invoke," "The Palace at 4 A.M.," "Make of Her Peril a Figure," "Diorama," and "The Book of Agatha."

Special thanks to Nikky Finney and the Poetry Society of America for awarding "The Book of Matthew" the Lucille Medwick Memorial Award.

1

Invoke

Bless me I am not myself. These days. Objects
pile on my work-bench: a flame. A seed. A heart. A brass
pig. A fat key. A creamer and pitcher also.
A number of benches have amassed a fleet
of flatnesses, some pew, some
not so pew, one with the names of tools carved
into the wood: PLANE   AWL   LEVEL   BRACE. What happens
when you are no one's shape. I'm stripping
paint. Where the meters
are all broken, find me.

Oracle Weather

I have found myself mostly sleepless in this strange place,
bewildered and restless, minus horses, absent magpies,
even the weather peculiar, though some say *upriver*—
their answer to everything. Mostly it's the lack of your body,
a sort of wilding, my hollows more hollow, the psalms
suddenly all about tempering. Upriver things get bigger,
they say, upriver the gods come down to the banks to drink
and those who watch are called twitchers, god-watching a jar
to the nervous system. Meantime day's a lousy container,
a porous happenstance in collusion with big weather.
The news here is largely of systems' overlap—woodpecker
lazarused back from oblivion, boy from the thick nightmare
of a man's hands. Ice on the power lines brings back
a silence I've been dying for want of. Upriver, someone says
at the bar, things get beautiful. That's not good enough.
My home brims with static. If you find a fossil, send it. Send
coral earrings. Send lotion. Poor dumbfounded day, I say
to day, the legs of the gods are thin as reeds and the systems
are failing spectacularly. Nerve-wired, I'll stay in. Should I
cut my hair short, should I vanish completely? Static's a winter
phenomenon, oracular: friction, sting. Shorn, I'll be braver.
Someone places a meaty hand on my thigh. He smells like
lime. Man is weak, you told me, and boatman weaker than
most, and thus I've come to say *dear* to the subtle nothing
of dusk. I want to believe any animal can be rendered into
usefulness, sustenance or slow-burning light, I want to believe
the throat is a slope we climb into shangri-las of whispering,
me saying *what* then leaning in closer. In my alley, a screen door,
gash in the mesh where something wanted in. The sculptor
has his crucible, I my list of figments. Alleyward, flotsam.

Inward, howling. Let the gods lap up what they will. Cream
clots in the dark. The branches thus fallen are glyphic yet
dumb. I'll smuggle new shoots under my raincoat, I'll nurse
your greenstick fracture. All the elkhounds are sleeping;
they have forests inside them, and quiet. Their coats are shiny
with proteins. Don't tell me you're not tired. The world
comes secondhand and I can live with this—rescued shelves
on which stones sit, breath first breathed by somebody else.

Keeper, Keeper

> *Ah, keeper, keeper, I have done these things*
> *That now give evidence against my soul.*
> — Richard III

Having bathed too long in near-scalding water
having laid down in the desert, dust in my clothes, charge to my spine
having known the fear of aviaries as a prayer
having not gone much of anywhere
having unsaid, but not unmouthed
having been the empty room's most perfect spouse

Sometimes soul seems
a vestige—like
dewclaws—of some
earlier order,
some phylum
under glass
for the docent
to talk about:
here is the iron thing
that recurred
throughout their little
world, dug up
with rusty nails
and bits of plastic.

Having bathed too long in near-scalding water
having, generally speaking, drunk too much
having not spoken for days, for days
having wholly shut up

I went to see the man who makes dolls from wisdom teeth.
Little tooth-heads.

Little robes, seed beads stitched on hems,
gold wire for bangles, the vestigial
a proper fetish,

little tooth-cowboy with his tooth-head
swinging his lasso

of braided fishing line.

Having gone looking for the smoothest stones
having seen the herons pterodactyl-ancient in the cottonwoods
having forged the icon inside some secret place
having been properly afraid
having thus resisted sleep
having meant no worldly harm
having zipped up the tent to keep warm

Coccyx, gooseflesh, the hollow bones
of flightless species; girlhood;
earlobes; the eyes of cavefish;

the way November's battered
on a blacksmith's anvil—Let me

live inside this uselessness a while longer.

Atomic Clock

I don't know why some people are shaped to a place, back to a ditch,
thighs to a stand of pines. Blame boy prophets. I mean bodily, absolutely.
I want rest, a little house, happy to shrink scale and vanish back into
the treeline. At the dog show, the announcer: "This is why I have my
cardiologist in the good seats, in the front row:" because it's so exciting.
On another channel, a lady swears *If they come inside my house again*
I'll shoot them dead, puffing up her chest to hide her fear of beautiful
boys with knives, of the place she's shaped by, saints among the azaleas
commanding *Stay here but arm thyself*. I've heard air leak from a girl's
throat, seen a man's body trembling in the dark. When I taste fear I
take a pill, or call my friend, or recite something in my head, *carpenter,*
carpenter, the world bucks and shifts, *tattered coat upon a stick,* the nor-
adrenaline kicks in. No bullet can do this thing you wish.

She loveth best who loves the strange birds trapped in Concourse B, flora day-glo and oversized, endless water, no slaughter *per se*, though, in a shop in one of the bleaker suburbs, a knife inlaid with meteorite, a knife inlaid with jet, a sapphire knife. Insects pinch my nerve ends. We fail and fail and grow desirous of believing we're all vehicle, every wet atom of us. You be the consort, says the man in the bar, I'll be your most faithful pet.

Isn't the park fantastic, corners pinned, its objects a floating hey-boathouse. The desert fathers and the desert mothers wonder what I'm doing here. A park's a dog-and-pony show, the husbands cannot stop jogging, always the unfaithful man walking his big white dog. I am a pioneer of time, pockets heavy with ticking, see the invasive come greenly o'er the pond. As the husbands scratch their heads. As the desert waits another age to take these acres down.

We have eaten the world and mean to keep swallowing. How *fall* attaches to *asleep*, how the boot slips on talused slopes—I'm done with meantime. I'm into ordinary time. No time like the river road, ice shoved up on ice. Stranger, *as we speak*. The air psalmic, which is to say charged. The air palmic, which is to say touched. So help me. But what if the world's not ending? Let's see.

Neither you nor I a shepherdess.

Not believing something doesn't make it less so. I could not believe in wolves but there'd still be one inside your pet. What a woman will do for thirst. What a throat will. My edges softened but something else was knapped, a pure obsidian. If hush was the first prayer and rose like a silo, what sort of silo. Tell me that, boy prophet. And so it came to pass that a woman looked me in the eye and said *I don't believe in ghosts but I saw one once.* This in the hallway of a building outfitted with plaster cherubim. I don't know why some people are shaped to a meridian, spine to a county, breasts to one man's hands. I mean bodily, absolutely. I want respite, a little room, spillways. The boy prophet's looking at a seeing-stone inside his hat, and from that saying when the horsemen are due back.

What a weird tenor this world is, how it lends the appearance of appearing like something else. And so there appeared in the appointed place at the appointed time a plaster angel. And the angel said I don't believe in girls but I saw one once. And the angel said I have never been a cormorant, never fell anywhere, let alone headlong. And the trees caught fire, wicking up and up. And thus did the rivers confluence: this one brown, this green, and unto that place a Forest Parkway, with Goodwill near the intersection of Arsenal & Kingshighway.

A creature scene in the dark. A water feature made on a lark. A theater: a park: a stage. A man-made lake. Which is not a lake. As bare is kin to not-there, the ragged dog on Waterman, fur falling out in great clumps, *Do you want to turn around and go back* and I said no, and now I carry him inside me like a clot of stopped time and no co-pay can buy me sleep. Sing to me, somebody.

Not thaw, not freeze, I wake in the air between, air thick with dimwitted pollen, spent chances. The old sirens sound closer but they're not; pre-melt, pre-runoff, what's unseen unanswering, the dog gone where, or hit by a car, or where. And who's to say's what's more like a temple, peeling signage or obese azaleas? Through the lattice partitioning self from sleep, through wandering sleep, I listen and imagine the partition meant to keep the angel clean while on level earth.

Who's to say what's more like a temple, windshield glass or full-throated ease? I know a woman obsessed with stopping time, transforming flux to a thing the hand might carry. *The beak that grips us.* Listen: a river cut the continent in half. The wilderness rose as incense. The spire lit up. The sky cracked open. I held my spirit in my hand; I put it back in; I heard it click.

I came to find what my body was shaped for, what prayer my shoulders pressed into, what *And so it was made so* was made so. And this is how I made away: by night, ironworks nothing but a poor dream; from air a wet cloth on my forehead; into ceaseless drought, the desert mothers and the desert fathers saying Leave your good things in the alley, leave your fine goods by the wayside, leave your costliest whatnots on the saint's wide avenue. If it's matter, it's rubbish; if it's tin, it's tinny to the ear, dear girl. And I folded back into mountains where beetles dig legs into hardwood and wait: a rot: a softening. Allegory of the Flammable Paradise: one by one the steeplejacks grew old.

The Book of Matthew

1.
She is painting the tree line again and again.
In this, her insides are scoured, she is able, after days
inside, to leave the studio, trade turpentine
for pine, for fenceposts. All I want
is to not stop walking
until I encounter a county where what's between houses
isn't alley. This sorrow has crept inside me like a spider
into my bed, like iris pollen sashaying
downstream, so fancy. The child outside my door
is not my child, just some random child
explaining the swimming pool. The dog outside my door
is not my dog, just some random dog
dragging his leash on the sidewalk.
Today the headline: Couple jumps off bridge
with son's body in rucksack.
At the tree line, the air tastes like ambrosia.
Far from the tree line, my dead return.
Where the fuck have you been?
But they're not sorry.
They say: Your problem isn't us,
your problem is that you're forever elegizing
the living, *the hair of my beloved is grayly gray*
and so forth. Then you curl up in a ball. Spideriris.
I sleep-sent the dead
graduation photos of their daughters.
In the image, the daughters stand in the desert,
ready to leap off of boulders.
As if they'll sprout hooves.

2.

The azaleas unfold with a violence
for which even this city's professional gardeners
aren't ready. Late storm, power lines down,
traffic lights out for miles, air pollinated
beyond reckoning, how the young stand around
in newly cut-off jeans and try to decide
if it means something.
This is the summer list: Lone Elk, Carmelite
novena, pregnancy test, Pink Sisters, confluence,
Thin Inn. One of those items comes first,
guess which. In another state, the painter
constructs a cabin from scrap metal. I have no idea
what *galvanized* means.
All May everyone felt particularly fated.
I believed I was meant to stop in a certain town
but kept driving, swore I was only love-struck
by all that barbed wire. Think of Simon Peter
frozen inside time, warming blue hands, shaking
not from the weather
but from the choice.
Have you ever frozen inside time, have you ever
stood warming your hands
while something cruel unfolded?
I'm doing it right now.

3.

I'm asking like a woman who needs to know.
In another state, the painter's snorkeling
in the Payette River, counting the sockeye salmon
for Fish and Game, mourning their peril.
She goes underwater, runs her palms
along the mossy undersides of stones, the light
bends away from her irises, her hands
numb, a sockeye comes into her sightline, she
sways, weightless,
has no idea what it's *like*, this eye so near her eye (a pink
novena? a secret? the end of time? No),
she climbs out, up the banks,
a truck in the distance
clangs over cattle grates,
clouds darken the water,
cones drop their seeds,
someone shakes out his sleeping bag,
someone slides her hands
up someone's thighs,
someone's lungs burn
from the thinning air,
someone says *I could have sworn*
your brother was there at the foot of the bed,
but when I woke—,
someone boils the jawbone,
stuffs their hands in their pockets,
someone squeezes river
from her hair,
makes a hatch mark

by the other hatch marks,
each of which represents
a creature seen in the dark.

4.

A sigh sounds dramatic but really
is just the scrubbing of lungs.
There's an airline called Air Comet,
why are you sad. In another state, the painter shakes pollen
into a mortar, paints a man with a beak.
Here, my friend says it's the Fin Inn, not the Thin Inn,
because there are fish in the walls.
My ears have been nothing but bother since I moved here.
I should have stopped in that barbed wire town,
stayed forever. Imagine the scrap metal available
at the slow edge of the desert
where everything takes decades to rust.
The man with the beak puts his hands on his hips.
I've seen crazed starlings trapped in the chapel, seen a magpie
hovering at eye level when I walked up the basement steps
into light that smelled like cilantro.
The man with the beak thrusts his hips
slightly forward.
I'm trying to avoid the nexus where I light out
and boom, before you know it there's another cabin
salvaged from dumpsters, slow-rusting, sure,
and like a drum when rarely rain comes,
that loud. Call it the Paradox of Barbed Wire:
on the one hand it smells exactly
like home, the Owyhee desert after rain.
Maybe there's a barb in my locket, and when I touch
its sharp edges I smell yarrow, and what's broken
inside me isn't so broken, mends
imperfectly as a wing mends, never again the same

but still useful. My lover's hand left a mark
on my collarbone, once. I know what I called it,
and I know what someone else
might have called it, had we met
in some gas station when I was headed West
and they, who knows.
On the other hand, you can use barbed wire
to tie a boy to a fence, leave him there as empire collapses
into a black hole
inside his beautiful eye.
Today the power lines genuflect
like the reverent, like someone doing cardio,
like light coming down to the river
to drink. Our violence tethered at our wrists
like some weird bird, we bend our heads
to drink from the ladle of our hands.

Seed Vault

Day comes in with a dungeon, out with a coo and a turgid moon. A woman, enterable, seems like stopgap for sorrow, sure, and yet I live alone, such blessings, the between a bleating offering its throat. Fluttering things have so distinct a shade! Glory the world unmade, glory the angel of silence, our S & M togetherness, our still life with bondage. I shoo him out, hum loudly; he stomps off, wings grazing cobwebs, at dusk sulks back and I lower my head and I thrum with frequencies below the lowest register. When my eardrums ruptured, he wrote *Baby you're mine now* on a slip of paper slivered through the keyhole, awful nothing-roar shaking the foundation. There are stalks full of bitter, he pleads, there are pods that, slit, give a milk so sweet a voice comes to seem catgut-cheap.

How boulder opals
hold their water

how all winter
my throat slammed shut

Hey opaline country
I'm over here now

fitful   rueful   unkempt

The little brass plaque on my door reads: Travelers & solicitors must ring bell. I mean to steal it when I move out. Listen: I've seen little girls in wedding cake dresses hand out carnations at the polling places, seen a guy on the corner of Grand & Arsenal say: *How do I know there're angels? I ain't never had one walk right up to me, shake my hand—*

Felted air,
power lines down—
no dial tone

One interesting expression is *Nothing's there*. I've quite the harem, ladies:
there's the angel of silence, and then there's the body I love best, who
resides on the other side of several mountain ranges.

Bestial weather and the dog
chained up

palm-sized book
burning in the oil drum

burning the anodyne spells

Propped up on my elbow, storm ghosting the trees, this is what I say to
the angel of silence: anodyne, poppy mine, the years a canyon without
looking down, the needlework-elaborate pattern storm-shifted, fragrant
as juniper: there the household boxed and sold, day a hinge I oiled and
oiled. A thousand kindnesses. Late rent. How I hitched up my skirts so
as not to snag on barbed wire; how herons made the river monstrous. I
abandoned one town, found another, turned at the three windmills, said
Holy the hail I'd FedEx by handfuls if I could as desert gave way to flash
flood and lightning kindled the foothills unto tinder. *Fantastic*, I said,
fantastic, and when called upon did supplicate: here is my underneath,
here is my best garden, here is what I've made in the gravest light while

my cells were rioting and my atoms were lighting the bonfires of the coming immolation, dizzy with the ordinary cruelties and wondering just who the seeds are being saved for, far north, encased below the permafrost.

> The desert a flash flood,
> a bewilderment;
>
> the desert a lost key,
> an astonishment

On a trip West, porn in the hotel room. I can take or leave it. The climax that puts me in the seats? World's end. Hail or locusts, freeze or thaw, I'm not picky. Like: last week I was late for lunch because I didn't want to miss the conflagration, fire rolling behind the credits. Eating everything.

> In my sleep
> the rangeland's burning
>
> and in my pocket
> a shard of obsidian
> from the world's last melting

Folly becomes us, the end of empire uncomfortable and strange, in the Walgreens' parking lot always someone with hand outstretched and I am stretched inside, drawn thin, more perplexed than anything, useless in this growing dim, incandescent lights replaced with little coils, blackout curtains meant to blank away the security lights that click on whenever someone passes, yard flooded with brightness all hours, night sky a blotted mess I must have dreamt once:

> Road to the mountain
> pocked with salt
>
> antediluvian
> boulders etched
>
> with spirals, arrows,
> constellations

I'm a woman waiting for world's end, assembling secondhand matter in lidded jars. Pods and such. Remnant glass. Prayer cards. I cut my hand—sharp tithe. In abandoned houses, women stir broth by the gallon, strain the bones. My beloveds are nothing I won't eat. See my icon? See my feast? Glacier's just a fancy term for sea. The world is the world's own eidolon.

> The last time I fired a gun
> the pure violence
>
> of the magpies' hyalescent
> scattering

Sleep's a dovecote with a tiny god in each hole, says the angel of silence. I tell him that my failings are daily are heavy are thickly crowding, a thicket a bramble a stain. And the angel of silence says I'm his goodliest wife, his prettiest helpmeet. I wash his feet, daydream pterodactyls knife-still in the locust trees, give good story: how, in the sanatorium—my lover told me this once, after he entered my body, after pulling out, after he said *If the light fixture were a constellation what constellation would it be*—in the sanatorium, men drowning in their own lungs would call out open windows to the women's ward above, obscene things, final wantings. This gladdens me enough that most days I get out of bed.

This wild need of yours/for wonder—

an alarm system so
I key in the proper code.

Corona Borealis, I say to the angel of silence, in case he's wondering. And the ruins, they're beautiful, and day is beautiful, a real Lazarus, a skinjob miracle. Collapse loneliness, get adoration, if you're lucky, boulevard redbud-blowsy, branch branch and shatter what the city wills of glass, silk lining rain-stained unto ghost blot amid these vinegar hours, this sour that begs: taste, taste, hosanna may we. What else is left?

2

Tinnitus

This is how time sounds, body
breaking down, river birds
dinosaurian. Who wouldn't pass out
outright, given plastic catching
rain, the lost chairs Orphan,
Smokebreak, Minor Mishap?
You think the park's the world
but the park's not the world,
it's not even a real view, the dream
of safety a sculpture garden,
a figment—a boy sleeps
on the riverbank, coat for a pillow.
Pelagic night, slight euphoria
of satellites, we blink lights
at each other. Let's make a shadow-
play of Lazarus: see the zombie
frown down at his weird suit
of skin. Like a glass rubbed
by a wine-wet finger, a hum inside
the prayer. Lung, lung, pull this cart
slowed up with sleep and touch.

Make of Her Peril a Figure

And where you plant the teeth, a city, mouth

of plate glass, forest parkway, intricacy

of thrift store distribution trucks and, through

this, our heroine, past the Christian Science

reading room, assault of azaleas

and the Furies in the ginkgos, watching.

The Furies in the ginkgos glow and know

signage: exit ramp, pawn shop, deer

crossing and the glyphs of boys, tags

more beautiful than neon breasts. Sweat

pools between her breasts; she is neither

waiting nor walking through a hole

in the cave wall. Go figure.

Make of her peril a figure, make a figurine, she

will build a diorama with stripped wires

hanging from empire chairs. Darling

an explosion is not the same as a meltdown says

the city. Tsk go the Furies. By the deli, a woman

sits on the grass with a kitten on a string.

A crop of men and arms. A crop of alley glass!

A crop of bug husks. I think this is meant

for small song. How a car door is like

a shield. How an alarm is like a bird: it circles,

moving out from its host then back again.

The heroine waves to the men in the leather

store, sits on a bench with her Pho and tracks

a Fury west past the boathouse towards the river.

O mighty barges, bring your brickloads closer.

Caught on the chainlink, milkweed; the pods

spill and colonize her lungs. And so she is flora.

Empire Coat

The eyes in the coat of empire

blink. World without end, globe
where the book, ulna
where the scepter, no

meteorologist like
the body. Storm seeps
through seams. Mouths
sewn to the coat of empire
gulp, sigh. Prayer

for men into battle:
                        Dear men

I have a very little power, I come
from altitudes where girl's
a godspeed wick and seas

melt their armadas
non. The city rusts. Regina, the ears
of your coat are burning, my gems

are thrifted, I have very little
power but hum
regally. *Why*

do you hum. I hum

because air's ermine. House made of
hands. Click stitched from
hummingbird skulls. Shoes

of small boats. Aftershock
like vertebrae's collapse. Bracelet

of throats like smokestacks
loving you with their bloom-
and-choke.

And in your coat I saw my fear: of
lakes, of snow, of the furs
of animals, ash
a pure contagion, body
in the lungs, of
crosswalks, of trees'
fleet human
shadows, of
ablutophobia, of
bays, how they enter
or, of the exited
body, always
the exited body, of
the eyes of
animals, have you seen
the eyes of
animals, of pill
dust, of barometer's
relentless pressure,

of day, comes
another, of the locket-
slight bones of
birds, of what the locket
holds (ash? nail
clippings? weather?) of half-
souls' blurred
voices, of
incandescence
gone and
then what, of the half-
life of strontium, of
radiation coating
the throat, of
coats' hollow
forms, of saints
creeping in and leaving
their gold
candles, of
mountains, my
god, of breaking, of
breaking, of
horses, of
sleeves, of pause—

Places I Haven't Slept

An island. The campground. In sixteen
states. At the sleep clinic, wanting
to strip the electrodes off
and glide home. Such feeble means: pill, wine, looped
sea sounds. In whatever bed
listening to breath, my body called
by what, jerking, muscles holding their animal
startle. By the Mississippi
in the house of sleeping women, barges
sliding past, my chest thick
with damp. The prophets thumbtacked to the walls
watching as I watched back.

Polysemy

> *What the world likes is a bootstrap and locket.*
> — Laura Jensen

Here is God, hazelnut
in one hand, Hey lady
in the other. His
calibrated love.

And in this he shewed me a lytil thyng the quantite of a hasyl nott. lyeng in
the pawme of my hand as it had semed. And it was as rownde as eny ball.

All observers are not led by the same physical evidence to the same pic-
ture of the universe.

I looked upon it with the eye of my understanding, and thought, 'What
may this be?'

He perceived linguistic differences to have consequences.

And it was answered generally thus, 'It is all that is made.'

We are parties to an agreement to organize it in this way.

She thought the world
was made of paper: step
on the street,
fall through.

When he says what he means
to do to my body, the sky
sinks into rangeland.
All the hotels in the universe
cannot raise it.
Having made my loneliness
my privacy, I don't remember
what to do with men.
Do you bathe them?
He says what he says about my inner thighs.
They still exist.

And God held out
his fists: guess
which. We stare.
Some see horses some
see cities. We
crave a punishment
and a keeping.
She was afraid
when it rained, that
the city would dissolve.

*She searched for a narrative that would explain why the world was being
transformed.*

Little ornaments.
I forget to speak all day

and poof!: something
turns up missing.
I buy a plumb bob
and a level—am seeing
how far down the hour.
"Should we stop and level things."
It's hopeless; it tilts,
this whole meridian.

I thought it might suddenly fall to naught for littleness.
It's quiet here.
The science of
locations, of creating names
through water
in water like
"jars of pond water":
tell them slow down
a figurative expression for slow down.
Sleep the grease
we apply to our bodies
to ease from thinking.

I have my styrofoam, my pins.

The communal eye
marks how the pinprick sun
blots out the moon.
The private eye
wonders when the world
will catch fire.
And all is tired and all is tired and all
sorts of matter shall
be tired.
Animals; the season.
We construct sadness
with vowels
between us,
a temporary storage.

Thrift

Stranger buying a sweater, what wool does to my skin
is little bumps. I am awkward with you here. Your
boots, my Pyrex. Outside, the horse
makes a wedge in air. I buy mercury glass, icicles
hung on strings. A saddle for the rodeo,
a pamphlet: *Is There a Prophet in Your House*? No.
This belt was something's skin. Three dollars.

Little Ornaments

1.
Not that I did not know fantasy; rather, that I reached
my life's equator with an understanding that certain
needs, when met, removed the necessity to dwell
on past or future; that if I slept without wedging
in the chasm, day would remain sufficient. So came
the equator. I walked its pencil line with arms outstretched,
unencumbered by husband or child, unmortgaged,
tethered to a certain region but otherwise content
to land—wherever. And landed in a brickwork city
where she dwelled discontent; she, whose fabulations
centered on land with proximity to water, grand
houses, and the scouting of real estate, wiping grime
off leaded panes to see flocked wallpaper. I have never
owned most variety of kitchen implements;
at the time of this writing, own exactly none. My needs
were met with admirable precision by an old riverman
back West, and by the mountains, which showed me up
as foolish whenever I thought of linear time.
At the time of this telling, currents track winter in.

2.
Because my dead were not yet dead, there was no need
to commune with them. I wanted to yell how the ballroom
would fall finally into the cellar, but, knowing uselessness,
sat on a bench and talked to a stray child and learned
the lock system by which the river remains level
as the barges displace tonnage—learned it so well
that I might even now, as party trick, construct

the system in miniature with shovel, garden hose,
and some toy boats. In any regard, when I slept
I dreamt, and thought, waking, of a notion no bigger
than that creditors might stop calling. When no sleep came,
I didn't think beyond the riverman; when the prophets
stared down from the walls of a rented house, they
seemed ill-groomed, not holy.

3.
She drove our expeditions, owing to my lack of navigational
wherewithal, my desire to wade into the Mississippi,
which enterprise would have slowed us down
considerably, currents being such a daft thing to collect—
better stamps, figurines. So: in such a manner
and with only a little vandalism, we saw the finest mansions
the bluffs had on offer, jangled doorknobs, admired
the tuckpointing, then drove home, me to a bare apartment
where what scarce visitors came were generally compelled
to stand through insufficiency of chairs; her to a coffin
of a house. It was the custom of that country to nail
the windows shut for protection, that amulet of enclosure
with which we are all familiar.

4.
What does that matter? Some do not distinguish the living
from the dead and so lived haunted. She held to signs,
such as crows tunneling from the sky meant certain
toothache, whereas I believed in the reversal of subject

and object brought by scale's enactment on the figure,
and a certain apocalypse not so much foretold as crafted
by large-brained monkeys. I thought the burnt-out church
installed with a thousand lamps (the number grows
in telling) said something of simple kindness, and that
the airstream lodged in the birch tops spoke to a happily
opiated maker, and that the temple was just another
purple, though I removed my shoes—which is all to say
that I have never in all my half-life stumbled on a house
and felt myself meant to live there. When I am lost—
as frequently—I feel it neurological, not godly; I pull over
and call for help; I scan the landscape for useful markers
and, finding none, wonder at all our foolishness, that—
boy prophets or no—we should drag ourselves across
a continent and build waystations amid such flatnesses.

5.
In this world, there are display cases lined with the skins
of yearlings holding gloves lined with the skins of yearlings.
I think fear our truest food. A brick that says Hydraulic;
Listo pencil leads; typewriter tins; slit pods of poppies;
wisdom teeth in specimen bottles. Some things I wear around
my neck, but don't pretend to know yoke from adornment.

6.
Water which previously pushed into tusks froze ragged,
the littoral species—shy, yolky—wintering elsewhere.
We ate and, I think, tipped well; we saw a yellow house,

a miniature holy village (blacksmith, aviary, pageantry,
prairie skirts). I'm conflating episodes like a plastic
telescoping cup, collapsing days together that I might
open up and stretch them, knowing it does not matter
in the grand—she would say scheme, I would say
mishap— . . . it does not matter in what season we hid
from nuns, in what season I lined the windows
with elixir bottles, or on what deck, sick with citronella,
a good woman mistook fireflies for shooting stars and
I saw finally how misapprehension need not frighten.

Diorama

See the cross-section opened on loss
so big you could charge admission? Hole
in the ceiling for the tree to grow through. Something
nests in the radiator. I don't climb up. I sleep
on the floor, thumb through the story of the woman
who disappeared. There is no sense
in fear of furniture. Even in my shaking,
love. Downstairs:
tin cabinets, chicken pot pie. We cannot
save anyone. At night, sleep
coming, my big eye peers into the house like so.

3

The Book of Agatha

An animal up close is frightening
if like us, frightening if not. Below certainty,

a word I cannot make out. Trouble with the hands, trouble

with the eyes, am the lit match? The burning
boat? The dowagers

recompose their spines with sounds

that say *I was this, now I am that.* Their cars
are cars of mystery. Agatha, where you're going

are drinks on a silver tray. Drink them.

Dreamt my feet in the lake, did I say, denim
hems heavy, how baptism

resembles drowning, assembles algae—

and the fox on the lake, if we feed him
will we be responsible, is that

what meat means—

I eavesdrop. Nest pushed from the gutter
by rain: ghost shells. Bird spit

keeps it perfect. Startle

a mink stole around my neck, some moments, yes,
I junkie-crave another

life, this one so swollen

with weather, with waters, the large and gentle

failures, husks
littering the highways—

Having given most everything away, save
skeleton keys and, for how it darkens, silver plate

bought on Cherokee Street: car full of women
yelling "bitch": my dowry:

I am making a practice of quiet. Pre-sleep

a slight chemical euphoria, and I remember

the police attending a friend's hallucinations:

Miss: Miss:

You can mudlark, if you'd like, and find the coins
of Roman emperors, sediment

seeping through your fingers—but today, Agatha,
you have taken the train

to Waterloo station; have checked into the hotel
under another name. In town, some sort of carnival;

someone walks out on the lake.

A number of theories have been advanced to explain this episode.

I think there was a flood—was fire—and now day

is a damage you wade into; how fearless: how
shaking. *So she rocked: so she shivered.* "There"

expressed as a clearing
from which the fox emerges, furnace-chest

regulating his temperature
so that restlessness does not set him on fire.

Doppelganger

Who nearly drowned was someone else.
To sit on your floor, hems dripping—

Who caved. Who wept. Bereft
and tired, tired. Leaves
burning in the next yard, weather
dragging. Or so I hear. I wasn't
there. Lungs full of algae. Throat
sore. To sleep on your floor, listening—

story of the woman who, coming
down, walked for a year,
past the railroad tracks, the bodega,
scoured as she entered the museum
and did slow laps around the hall
of miniatures, the paradise

painted with a Q-tip, the adjuration
leaking from the frame.

Implanted Memories

You were the finest circus, swallowing fire
like that. And when the river flooded,
you stepped out the second story window
and rowed away. No danger so great-big
you did not rise to greet it, hello, skirts
bobbing like altostratus. How the old men
wept into your soup; how the hawk
took your wrist as the steadiest branch. Fear another
province, how the dead left absolute signs
on the sill: greeting cards, bent tines, snow.

Vernal, Utah

I am never lonely there. I sling hash, groom
horses, step from one life into another,
selves falling from me like fire-coats, like
kilowatts. Last night I woke from a cold
sweat: Vernal or never, Vernal or bust.
Have I mentioned how I'm not alone there?
I rent rooms to ornithologists
and sculptresses. They sigh in their pleasant
sleep. We take turns washing up.

The Palace at 4 A.M.

After Giacometti

Desire a winding spine, a dress form, this
scaffolding from which frail legs swing.
I saw you through a quivering sheet of glass.
You were the filmstrip where the man
balances on a wire between burning
centuries, you were the reel where monks,
inscrutable, refuse to speak for years, touching
each other in the dark to know the hem

of God. And who's to say the dinosaur bird
has no place in our darkest want? I grow
ancient. My bones matchstick. The world
was burning and is burning still. And who's
to say the dressed form draws any luck from
its finest wool? I say it only catches faster.

Sea Voyage

On its sea voyage, my locket
moves toward me. A tusk,
a birdfish in the cargo hold.
The gulls and such, their
hunger. Recorded data:
noon, locket closer. Why
countenance foundering?
Waiting coos at my feet.
The newspaper thuds
on the mat, but I'm too busy
thinking about the locket.

I don't understand blind faith
or how much salt is in the sea.
The ship's propelled by
algorithim, robot arm.
The sea was darkness; after
the sea, time. The birdfish
washes its feathers.
I ignore the weather channel.
The sky dresses as sea,
which complicates everything.
I don't know where to look.

Wanting to be productive,
I bought the locket. We're
only here, we firmament,

to divide the waters
from the waters.
A man on the radio
says his parents are dead
so he touches iridium,
tungsten, copper.
When the world clicks
against the magnet, his face
lights up. Go ahead, search it.

I check the tracking number.
Waiting makes the hour
far down. The locket
has a little window so
what's inside might peer
out. I feel like an automaton
whose function is to sit here.
I see the locket as sensible
compromise between this privacy
and the new yelling
everyone's doing.

The sky gets in my clothes.
The fireplace stars
small apocalypses.
Across the sea,
the goldsmith rubs her eyes.

In the Exclusion Zone

After the world ends, the old women come back to sift ashes. Icons nailed to the barns fold flawless hands. Our feet are tired, say the women. Should've thought of that, say the icons. The women tsk. Sore before, sore after.

When the world was ending, liquidators came. Their shoes dissolved in standing water.

Summer of wild boars rooting through squash and skeletal houses. Somewhere, another world is ending. Those old women will have to glue it back together too, a dropped saucer, shards wobbling in space.

A thousand miles north, a boy wills his legs to jump from ice to ice. When he looks down, he sees the underside of longing. What his muscles know about the sea would make you weep. He wears a seal hat, chews seal fat to stay awake.

One old woman wets a handkerchief, bathes her neck. The sound a wolf makes on the edge of the wood is no different than the sound it makes inside you.

For centuries men gathered in forests and prayed for this, tongues lolling, God staining them with sweat and a song: *firesheet hooves oh baby lava tinder.*

The women eat fiddleheads despite all warnings. Elsewhere, the sea gyres keep gyreing till they become their own gravity, their own garbage-weather.

Once, in the history of the world, a boy and his friends decided to be an orrery. *Calliope*, he said, arms out from his sides, spinning through the schoolyard, fixed to an older boy-planet yet weighty with himself. Until, for a millisecond, he tilted outside time.

At first, the old women were relocated to concrete tenements in distant cities. They built nests of telephone wire, of threads pulled from their sleeves.

Bigger than a bread box, the oil drums burn and burn.

Letter to a Young Poet

Do whatever it takes to rest. When sorrow
sits on your chest, give him a lick. I have no clue
if I'm old or young. I think you're a young lady
who should know I've never been to a castle,
though I did spend a day at the Climatron and,
after, scooped lotus pods from the mud. They
didn't dry well. I wish you well. It's possible
for a year to forget where it left itself. Don't
worry. The trees immolate. My waking dreams
involve shoeing horses, pounding silver sheet
into a lake. "A match burning in a crocus": I'd feed
children to wolves to be so precise. My house
blinks all night with small lights. I know you know
what I mean. I love incandescence the way
some women love God. Where you are, is it
gone? Do all the lights hum in sad tubes? I seam
the hour to the hour, flee parties like a woman
might flee killer bees. Go to sleep. Was a girlhood,
some hitchhiking, a man like a Viking stirring
polenta on an island in another century several
cataclysms ago: blink of an eye. Take the State
for a patron, but not for a wife. If sometimes
I seem not here, it's not dreaminess; it's fear.
If sometimes I don't hear, it's not celestial
ringing, but this inner ear thing I've had since
I lived in the city. At Babel, all the workers
knew the Milky Way spread like fat between meat
but felt zero need to say so. Look at something
till your eyes burn. *Pitcher plants drown
their prey:* not euphemism. The kettle's burning.

A woman felt called by don't-know-what
scratching like plumeria inside her. *Abide, abide*
says alluvial time. Trickster, long con, light
throws its nets over the yard. These words reek
of eucalyptus, bathtub gin. When the sky
turns absinthe, take cover. Say you're watching
the play where the woman turns into a tree and
suddenly, first act: tornado sirens. Her soul is sap.
Water pools on the floor. Ask yourself: do I love
the woman I'm sitting with? Don't get gyred into sky.
It's lonely there. Listen: the book is always burning.
So's the city. The water on stage is prop water,
can't put out anything. Blink if you can hear me.

Foretold

If the trees bend, you will startle soon. I do my best work
inside a hearty Go Away. I grow ashamed and vow.
The shame becomes fever, sweats through the sheets,
runs out to sea. My shame a sort of jellyfish, underwater
parasailor. And all this time I'm working, trying not
to become some desert parable: the beehive structures,
the epigrams. The sad garments, the love so big
birds won't come near. The quiet. The force field.

Ecophilia

The houses recursive but frail.
I rest between breath and sky, I sky
a lot, someone says why
are you always out here, under the branches.
Seeing carves the storm in wax.
Here is weather around my neck, silver thing
half flame half seed.

When I looked into day and knew that what came next
was, inevitably, flood—

Like a pill or radium, my half-life.
There are sky preserves where's stitched a hem (like a yard)
and light sewn in.
There are preserves in crawlspaces
put up for world's end, peaches
lobed and floating.
In the next county, a machine for squeezing cattle:
that they may feel, before the final terror, love.

When I looked into day and knew
that what came next was, inevitably, flood—

Ash sifts through locust trees, means to settle my eye.
Where is the darkest sky.
How to abandon the comfort
of vigilance, the worldfire burning?
I do not mean to pray: the apostasy of speech.

When I looked into day
and knew that what came next was, inevitably, flood—

Shell, and rind, and bark.
In sleep, Lucretius says, the spirit wanders.
Someone threads a reed
down the storm petrel's throat, restless lamp
that burns and burns.

My body curls like a fiddlehead
inside the dream of safety.
In the next county, my spirit lies down in the orchard.
My fear marries the public fear.
Throat sugared, dusk coming on.
I keep the yard like a paramour.

When I looked into day and knew that what
came next was, inevitably,
flood—

I move toward rough kindness.
Monger, monger, these girls
walking by the railroad tracks
have never heard of you.

All the Way from Here

Wool sky I am exhausted by, wool throat, river's skin
of ice, time stoppered in the city of trees where painted
men root for—something. Let the cruel be cruel,
let volcanic ash be hawked in canning jars outside
the grocery store. The mailman shivers. Long story
short, I don't miss what I've lost, half-souls with a blur
in their voice; it was Climatron and we were scientists
of sleep, the tired tech, the measurements. Women
stored tropical birds in townhouses and I could not
save them. On cruise control we drove the saint's
wide avenue. These days, the desert fathers
and the desert mothers wildfire through my sleep,
take no shit, think steeplejacks are boys who've never
spent the night outside. Scrapmetal drags along
the highway and the county conflagrates, my silence
metallurgical, signal seared away till what's left shines
like pyrite scavenged in old mining towns, green-gold
and daft. If I were a priest, I'd kill something and beg
the world to start again. So many among us aren't
among us, so many beside us are missing as barbed wire
unsutures from field, and I walk out in the city
of trees, and the hawk screams, and the smaller birds
perch nearby as though handmaids to an oracle.
Slipshod amygdala assembled by a clumsy lord,
spinster in the hands of a fussy god, I give away
my startle and the geography *does not disappear*,
the clerks are kind, the great rivers hum along, ice-clotted
or clear. I go out among a field of antlers spread
on bedsheets, yard sale at the top of the hill, I go out
among this grand diminishment of time, this

usury: geraniumed room, hooved caller. Green
seeing, stab-stitchery. And do I swoon? I swoon. And
the bodies moved into, through—shared vagaries.
To pretend otherwise would make me a shouting child.

Postscript

We looked for golden birds. We looked and looked.
We issued threat advisories. Our survival kits

were beautiful: tin, tin, pocket mirrors, root foods,
anodynes. We buried our seeds deep, we lined our bibs

with lead. Oh darling, we said, and rubbed a little bit.
We rode our fine horses, our sad horses, we sounded

the ram's horn and waited. Wanted. Rubbed cloves
on painful gums. Split the creature, crawled inside.

Told gorgeous lies. Catalogued the footed species.
Example: mastodon. In burnt-out churches, installed

pink lights that hummed and hummed. Bought
water rights. Visited the tombs, placed our rubbings

inside spiral notebooks. Stored everything we could.
Example: mercury. Chewed mint. Tooled leather

with desert flowers. Said leather when it was not
our skin. Drank from the river again. Inked our wasp-

papery outsides. Example: Om. Increasingly
did not wish to be alone. Said this mark means this.

Said this mark means. Said the moon a sliver. The moon
a hook. Shackled men to chairs. Tongued the rind.

Made our ponchos watertight. Loved string, the way
it marshalled points into a line. Were thoughtless. Thought

of nexts. Rinsed, spit. Pocketed. Rubbed more. Knew
what crepe was for, how to shoe a horse. Had names

for everything. Example: farrier. Thought trees
were weeds and pulled them up. Screwed men in canvas

tents. In brocade tents. In woolen tents. In tents so
shantung, no memory could hold them. Sieved metal.

Skimmed a little off the top. Said bottoms up and
swallowed. Leaned in real close. Carded wool. Etched

spirals, initials, dates from one calendar or another
onto metamorphic boulders. Had a site called Sharpening

Made Easy. Took the train. Burnt blessings. Wrung
the loon's neck. Said poor thing and would you look

at that. Looked at that. Put the loaf on the radiator to rise.
Drank the yeasty smell. Drifted through Aztec time.

Jangled keys as we traipsed through cells. Through canyons.
Through the valley. Of the shadow. Knelt. Knelt. Knelt.

Used a rasp, a wet grinder, a Phillips-head. Wasted
what was left. Steeped moss. Sucked aspirin from the bark.

Redacted. Tied boys to barbed wire with barbed wire.
Were proud. Stuttered. Example: the the the and so forth.

Dipped the sponge in vinegar. Dipped the crusts in wine.
Anointed every inch. Set the torch alight. Logged off. Came

close as light grew thin. Squinted the world to blur. Left
plastic flowers by the roadsides. Ate snow. Combed the dog

for burrs. Tied knots. Walked where heat fused sand to glass.
Forgot. Did not forget. Said outer space. Were kingly fools.

Were broke. Were broken. Tried to image ghosts. Measured
the particulates. Said what does that mean. And what does

that. Rubbed oil into our hips. Hands on our hips. Our hips
lifted to meet our hips, we gnawed the world's bones clean.

Notes

1

"Keeper, Keeper" references the work of artist Larry Krone.

In "Atomic Clock" the phrase "carpenter, carpenter" comes from George Oppen; "tattered coat upon a stick" quotes William Butler Yeats; "full-throated ease" belongs to John Keats; "The beak that grips us" paraphrases Adrienne Rich's "The beak that grips her, she becomes"; "I held my spirit in my hand" is from Elizabeth Barrett Browning's *Sonnets from the Portuguese* ("I cannot teach my hand to hold my spirit so far off"); the phrase "Flammable Paradise" is indebted to Laura Jensen. The poem also owes debts to JoAnna Novak and Amy Baily.

In "Seed Vault" the line "Fluttering things have so distinct a shade" belongs to Wallace Stevens and "This wild need of yours / for wonder" belongs to Craig Arnold.

2

In "Tinnitus," "Orphan, Smokebreak, Minor Mishap" are titles of three photographs from Bill Keaggy's book *50 Sad Chairs*.

"Make of Her Peril a Figure" owes its inspiration to Ovid: "He sows the teeth at Pallas's command, / And flings the future people from his hand. / The clods grow warm, and crumble where he sows; / And now the pointed spears advance in rows; / Now nodding plumes appear, and shining crests, / Now the broad shoulders and the rising breasts; / O'er all the field the breathing harvest swarms, / A growing host, a crop of men and arms" (Allen Mandelbaum, translator).

The poem "Empire Coat" references Elizabeth I's *Rainbow Portrait*, painted by Isaac Oliver, circa 1600.

The poem "Polysemy" quotes extensively from Julian of Norwich and the Sapir-Whorf hypothesis. "She searched for a narrative that would explain why the world was being transformed" and the image of a world constructed of paper are from the article "Which Way Madness Lies" by Rachel Aviv, *Harper's*, December 2010.

The title "Little Ornaments" comes from the final chapter of Nathaniel Hawthorne's *The Scarlet Letter*. The poem references the piece "Chorus" in the Light Project by artists Spencer Finch, Sebastian Hungerer, Rainer Kehres, Ann Lislegaard, and Jason Peters.

3

In "The Book of Agatha," the line "A number of theories have been advanced to explain this episode" is quoted from Joan Acocella's August 16, 2010 *New Yorker* article, "Queen of Crime: How Agatha Christie Created the Modern Murder Mystery." The dowagers are borrowed from *Mrs. Dalloway*, as is "*So she rocked: so she shivered.*"

"Sea Voyage" is inspired by the work of metalsmith Julia Vine. The line "When the world clicks / against the magnet, his face / lights up" is from an Oliver Sacks video: www.sciencefriday.com/videos/watch/10338.

"In the Exclusion Zone" is named for the area around Chernobyl.

In "Letter to a Young Poet," the line "A match burning in a crocus" is from *Mrs. Dalloway*.

In "Ecophilia," the image of storm petrel as lamp comes from Jane Brox's *Brilliant: The Evolution of Artificial Light.* The poem references Lucretius's *De Rerum Natura.* The line "I do not mean to pray" belongs to May Swenson.

I wish to express my deepest gratitude to Carl Phillips, Mary Jo Bang, and all my colleagues and students at Washington University. Special thanks to Brian Teare and to Jane Mead.

IOWA POETRY PRIZE AND
EDWIN FORD PIPER POETRY AWARD
WINNERS

1987
Elton Glaser, *Tropical Depressions*
Michael Pettit, *Cardinal Points*

1988
Bill Knott, *Outremer*
Mary Ruefle, *The Adamant*

1989
Conrad Hilberry, *Sorting the Smoke*
Terese Svoboda, *Laughing Africa*

1990
Philip Dacey, *Night Shift at the
    Crucifix Factory*
Lynda Hull, *Star Ledger*

1991
Greg Pape, *Sunflower Facing the Sun*
Walter Pavlich, *Running near the End
    of the World*

1992
Lola Haskins, *Hunger*
Katherine Soniat, *A Shared Life*

1993
Tom Andrews, *The Hemophiliac's
    Motorcycle*
Michael Heffernan, *Love's Answer*
John Wood, *In Primary Light*

1994
James McKean, *Tree of Heaven*
Bin Ramke, *Massacre of the Innocents*
Ed Roberson, *Voices Cast Out to Talk
    Us In*

1995
Ralph Burns, *Swamp Candles*
Maureen Seaton, *Furious Cooking*

1996
Pamela Alexander, *Inland*
Gary Gildner, *The Bunker in the
    Parsley Fields*
John Wood, *The Gates of the
    Elect Kingdom*

1997
Brendan Galvin, *Hotel Malabar*
Leslie Ullman, *Slow Work through
    Sand*